I'M DONE WITH
EITHER/OR THINKING AND LIVING
WORKBOOK

Erica Renée

Table of Contents

Dedication

I dedicate this book to my amazing mom, Brenda L. Ford, that I miss more than I thought humanly possible. I watched her slip away on October 6, 2016. Although she knew it would happen one day, she did not get the opportunity to see me become an author. When she was naming me in the hospital, the thought came to her, "Erica Renee would be a great name when she is an author." And so it was the name placed on my birth certificate. This is why instead of using my last name, I have chosen to be known to my literary audience by my first and middle.

I will dedicate every book to you because you dedicated your life to me. I love you more than words can express. I am the woman I am today because of you and I will always be grateful for your self-sacrificing love and friendship. If I am half the woman you were, I will have accomplished something great. I look forward to seeing you again. Bye for now.

Acknowledgements

I want to acknowledge my wonderful husband Sean R. Moore who is my best friend. You have been such a blessing to me during the process of birthing this workbook, and I will always be grateful for your support.

My awesome book editor LaToya Thompson for helping me flush out my thoughts to create something impactful.

My meticulous book cover art designer and formatter, Rey Contreras Jr. for helping me to produce a quality, top shelf product.

My BFF Oshea Vega for being the sister I never had.

My four amazing children: Heaven, Sean, Isaiah, and Hannah for bringing laughter into my life.

My God who is my everything.

A Note from Erica Renée

Hello!

I am so thrilled that you have this workbook in your hands. Not only does this mean that you understand the importance of your thought life but that you are willing to take the steps necessary to ensure that you cultivate and maintain a healthy mentality. Congratulations on coming to that conclusion. That is half the battle. In order to do better we must know better.

For as he thinks in his heart, so is he. (Prov. 23:7a AMPC)

This workbook will help you to examine your heart. The second King of Israel, David prayed, "Lord give me a clean heart." (Ps. 51:10)

As you delve into your soul, (mind, will, and emotions) through the exercises in this book, you may see some things you like and dislike. It is important that you resist the urge to edit yourself. Be as honest as possible as you answer the questions. This is for your benefit. Treat this workbook like a journal only to be seen by you, God and whomever you will entrust it with. This workbook can be used in small group settings to foster accountability, authentic relationship and healthy community.

You will be asked to think about some things you may have forgotten about, repressed or even regret. This is not to bring shame or condemnation on you but to free you from the power of whatever may have held you down or might be holding you down right now.

Then you will know the truth, and the truth will set you free. (John 8:32 NIV)

You may be asking yourself, "Why is this book so thick?" Let me assure you, I was surprised myself when I saw how large it was. But as I began to delve into my heart and type my daily process for mind renewal and heart health, the pages just kept going and going. This book is thick because its goal is transformation.

I didn't want to produce a resource that would just skim the surface. I wanted to create an experience that you could use to detox your heart and mind of everything that pollutes while also providing you with the supplements needed to rebuild things that may have been broken or damaged through just living your life. And even if life has been great so far, I wanted to give you tools necessary to maintain your mental and internal stability no matter what the future brings. I also wanted to ensure that it was large enough for you to record all of your thoughts in one place, rather than having to do so in a journal or a device.

I understand this workbook may be thick and cumbersome and not easy to take with you unless you have a large bag, but I believe you will find it to be useful. Sure, some exercises will more than likely be difficult to complete. You may even get annoyed with me and want to chuck the book across the room. No worries! I wanted to chuck my computer a few times while typing. And some of the exercises were challenging for me to complete. Some required intense thought, and some I had to skip and come back to later. It's not always the comfy and cozy conversations that bring enlightenment. Oftentimes, it's the difficult ones. So if it gets difficult to complete an exercise, don't give up. Burrow through it because it's only when muscles tear during a workout that they begin to grow.

This workbook is designed to help you grow. So get some coffee, water, tea and your favorite snack. Block out some space in your schedule perhaps once a week or even daily to allow God to speak to you as you ask Him to reveal you to you.

Don't be embarrassed if you don't know how to answer a question. There is no shame in taking several days to do so or in having to skip certain exercises only to return later. Your process is your process. Enjoy it, embrace it, and grow from it.

Think BIG, Live BIG,
Erica Renée

How To Work The Workbook

This workbook is designed to accompany my books, _I'm Done With Either/Or Thinking_ and _I'm Done With Either/Or Living_. Each chapter in the workbook was created with the content of both books in mind. While you can still benefit from going through the workbook without having read either _I'm Done With Either/Or Thinking_ or _I'm Done With Either/Or Living_, it is recommended that you do read one or both first or along with the workbook so as to have a deeper understanding of the concept of **Either/Or** thinking and how to become free from it. Both books are available at _ericarenee.co_.

The goal of this workbook is to further assist you in living a limitless life as you serve the limitless God. You may complete it in a month or less or it could take you an entire year. One is not better than the other. My hope is that you don't just work the workbook but that you allow the workbook to work within you. The workbook is comprised of several exercises to help you walk out the principles taught in both **Either/Or** books. Should you run out of space as you are writing, there are additional pages toward the back of the workbook. Let's get started!

Chapter 1: What Are My Either/Or Thoughts?

Introduction

In this chapter, you will learn what **Either/Or** thoughts are so that you can properly identify them. Once identified, you will progress through the workbook to dismantle them and replace them with the right thoughts.

Overview

An **Either/Or** Thought or **Either/Or** Thinking is designed to place limitations on what we think God, others, and even we ourselves can do, receive, and achieve. This thought follows the premise that in order for one area of our lives to flourish, another area must suffer. It's thinking that we simply can't accomplish more than one desire at the same time.

Some examples of **Either/Or** Thoughts:

- I can **Either** put in long hours at my job, and be successful, **Or** I can spend more time with my child and be a good parent.
- I can **Either** have a great social life **Or** focus on my relationship with God.
- I can **Either** be a bored, secure employee, **Or** I can be a happy, broke artist.
- I can **Either** accept the person interested in me now, **Or** I can wait and possibly never have an intimate relationship, because there may not be a better option out there.

Exercise

What are your **Either/Or** Thoughts? List them in the following categories

Financial

Example: I can **Either** work around the clock and skip all of my vacation time and have no social life, **Or** I will never make enough money to live comfortably.

1. I can **Either** _____**Or**

_____

2. I can **Either** _____**Or**

_____

3. I can **Either** _____**Or**

_____

4. I can **Either** _____**Or**

_____

5. I can **Either** _____**Or**

_____

6. I can **Either** _____**Or**

_____

7. I can **Either** _____**Or**

_____

8. I can **Either** _____**Or**

_____

9. I can **Either** _____**Or**

_____

10. I can **Either** _____**Or**

_____

Spiritual

Example: I can **Either** pray and read my Bible daily, **Or** I am not a good Christian.

1. I can **Either** _____ **Or**

_____

2. I can **Either** _____ **Or**

_____

3. I can **Either** _____ **Or**

_____

4. I can **Either** _____ **Or**

_____

5. I can **Either** _____ **Or**

_____

6. I can **Either** _____ **Or**

_____

7. I can **Either** _____ **Or**

_____

8. I can **Either** _____ **Or**

_____

9. I can **Either** _____ **Or**

_____

10. I can **Either** _____ **Or**

_____

Children and Parenting

Example: I can **Either** have children before I am 35 years old, **Or** I will never have them.

1. I can **Either** _____ **Or**

_____

2. I can **Either** _____ **Or**

_____

3. I can **Either** _____ **Or**

_____

4. I can **Either** _____ **Or**

_____

5. I can **Either** _____ **Or**

_____

6. I can **Either** _____ **Or**

_____

7. I can **Either** _____ **Or**

_____

8. I can **Either** _____ **Or**

_____

9. I can **Either** _____ **Or**

_____

10. I can **Either** _____ **Or**

_____

Spouse

Example: I **Either** have to compromise my standards in order to attract a spouse, **Or** I can stay true to my standards and stay single.

1. I can **Either** _____**Or**

_____

2. I can **Either** _____**Or**

_____

3. I can **Either** _____**Or**

_____

4. I can **Either** _____**Or**

_____

5. I can **Either** _____**Or**

_____

6. I can **Either** _____**Or**

_____

7. I can **Either** _____**Or**

_____

8. I can **Either** _____**Or**

_____

9. I can **Either** _____**Or**

_____

10. I can **Either** _____**Or**

_____

Health

Example: I can **Either** eat what I want and enjoy my food, **Or** I can eat what I should and not enjoy my food.

1. I can **Either** _____**Or**

_____

2. I can **Either** _____**Or**

_____

3. I can **Either** _____**Or**

_____

4. I can **Either** _____**Or**

_____

5. I can **Either** _____**Or**

_____

6. I can **Either** _____**Or**

_____

7. I can **Either** _____**Or**

_____

8. I can **Either** _____**Or**

_____

9. I can **Either** _____**Or**

_____

10. I can **Either** _____**Or**

_____

Career/Purpose

Example: I can **Either** get a job in a field I know will provide security for my family, **Or** I can pursue my passion and risk poverty.

1. I can **Either** _____**Or**

_____

2. I can **Either** _____**Or**

_____

3. I can **Either** _____**Or**

_____

4. I can **Either** _____**Or**

_____

5. I can **Either** _____**Or**

_____

6. I can **Either** _____**Or**

_____

7. I can **Either** _____**Or**

_____

8. I can **Either** _____**Or**

_____

9. I can **Either** _____**Or**

_____

10. I can **Either** _____**Or**

_____

Social Life/Friendships

Example: I can **Either** compromise my standards to please and attract friends, **Or** I can hold to my standards and be lonely.

1. I can **Either** _____**Or**

_____

2. I can **Either** _____**Or**

_____

3. I can **Either** _____**Or**

_____

4. I can **Either** _____**Or**

_____

5. I can **Either** _____**Or**

_____

6. I can **Either** _____**Or**

_____

7. I can **Either** _____**Or**

_____

8. I can **Either** _____**Or**

_____

9. I can **Either** _____**Or**

_____

10. I can **Either** _____**Or**

_____

Extended Family

Example: I can **Either** convert all of them to Christianity, **Or** I cannot associate with them at all.

1. I can **Either** _____**Or**

_____

2. I can **Either** _____**Or**

_____

3. I can **Either** _____**Or**

_____

4. I can **Either** _____**Or**

_____

5. I can **Either** _____**Or**

_____

6. I can **Either** _____**Or**

_____

7. I can **Either** _____**Or**

_____

8. I can **Either** _____**Or**

_____

9. I can **Either** _____**Or**

_____

10. I can **Either** _____**Or**

_____

Other

1. I can **Either** _____**Or**

_____

2. I can **Either** _____**Or**

_____

3. I can **Either** _____**Or**

_____

4. I can **Either** _____**Or**

5. I can **Either** _____**Or**

_____

6. I can **Either** _____**Or**

_____

7. I can **Either** _____**Or**

_____

8. I can **Either** _____**Or**

9. I can **Either** _____**Or**

_____

10. I can **Either** _____**Or**

_____

Chapter 2: Where Did These Either/Or Thoughts Come From?

Introduction
In this chapter, you will be asked questions to help you identify where your **Either/Or** thoughts originated from so that you can eliminate the source.

The thief's purpose is to steal, kill and destroy.
My purpose is to give life in all its fullness. (John 10:10 TLB)

Overview

God is a limitless God and doesn't place limitations on our thinking. Any form of limited thinking comes from the thief, Satan, the devil, who is our enemy. Jesus came as described in the above verse to give us life in abundance. And a Christlike mind is a mind that thinks abundantly.

So Satan is the source of **Either/Or** thinking, and he appears in our lives through various forms and influences. He appeared in the form of a snake to Eve in the garden of Eden but came to Jesus through Peter, a trusted friend and disciple. He makes suggestions to our minds through words and our imaginations.

Also, different life experiences could have planted **Either/Or** thoughts in our minds without us even knowing it. The following list is not exhaustive but does include some of the influences through which **Either/Or** thoughts may have been planted in our minds:

- Family tradition or expectations
- Words spoken to you or about you
- Words you have spoken over yourself
- Cultural norms
- Societal norms in your environment
- Media/arts or entertainment
- Workplace/field expectations
- Traumatic experiences or violations

It's hard to serve the limitless God when we have limited thinking.

Exercises

Exercise 1: Taking the above list into consideration, what are the top 3 influences that you believe **Either/Or** thoughts came or come to you? List them here. If it is something not listed, list it below.

1) _____
2) _____
3) _____

Exercise 2: Using the top 3 influences that you believe **Either/Or** thoughts came or come to you, answer how you will avoid or limit your exposure to that influence. An example has been provided to guide you. Example:

> Q1) How can you avoid or limit your exposure to the influence you wrote on line 1?
> A1) I selected Media/arts and entertainment. I will refrain from listening to sexually charged music and will only watch the news for 30 minutes or less a day and not before bedtime.

Your turn:

1) How will you avoid or limit your exposure to the influence you wrote on line 1?

_____
_____
_____
_____

2) How will you avoid or limit your exposure to the influence you wrote on line 2?

_____
_____
_____
_____

3) How will you avoid or limit your exposure to the influence you wrote on line 3?

_____
_____
_____
_____

Even if your circumstances don't change, they will change when you do.

Exercise 3: Sometimes it is not possible to limit exposure to the influences of **Either/Or** thoughts, such as the influence of a spouse or a living situation that you cannot immediately remove yourself from. Answer the following questions to discover a step toward freedom.

1) What will you do on a regular basis to ensure that you are strong mentally, spiritually, emotionally, and physically so you maintain your internal stability when you are in contact with the influence on line 1?

_____

_____

_____

_____

_____

2) What will you do on a regular basis to ensure that you are strong mentally, spiritually, emotionally, and physically so you maintain your internal stability when you are in contact with the influence on line 2?

_____

_____

_____

_____

_____

3) What will you do on a regular basis to ensure that you are strong mentally, spiritually, emotionally, and physically so you maintain your internal stability when you are in contact with the influence on line 3?

_____

_____

_____

_____

_____

Exercise 4: Choosing to avoid or limit your exposure from an unhealthy influence means that you can choose to spend your time and energy on a healthier influence. With this in mind, answer the following question. An example has been provided to guide you.

Example: Q) How will you spend your time and energy now that you have limited your exposure to the influences listed in Exercise 1? Think of activities, habits, persons, or events that can help you on your journey to freedom.

A) Influence 1: Media/arts and entertainment. Now that I am not listening to sexually driven music, I will listen to faith-filled Christian music at the times I normally would have played the other music. And with the extra time I have since I'm watching the news less, I'll listen to a podcast or audiobook on faith or a subject concerning me.

Your turn:

Q) How will you spend your time and energy now that you have limited your exposure to the influences listed in Exercise 1? Think of activities, habits, persons, or events that can help you on your journey to freedom.

1) Influence 1:

_____

_____

_____

_____

_____

2) Influence 2:

_____

_____

_____

_____

_____

3) Influence 3:

_____

_____

_____

_____

_____

Wrap up/Challenge

Consistency is important when making lifestyle changes. Review what you wrote in Exercise 4. What changes can you realistically make today and continue for the next 30 days? Get an accountability partner who will encourage and support you on your freedom journey. I challenge you to begin making this shift immediately and be consistent for 30 days. After that, you'll find it easier to maintain the new habit even after that time has passed.

YOU CAN DO IT!

Chapter 3: Getting Christ's Mind

Introduction
In this chapter, we will take a closer look at the mind of Jesus Christ and how we can let His mind be in us.

Who has known the mind of the Lord so as to instruct him?
But we have the mind of Christ. (1 Cor. 2:16 NIV)

Overview
The Bible, which is the Word of God, is a mirror. The Holy Spirit's job is to help us to reflect the image of Jesus Christ who we see reflected in the Scriptures.

While Jesus was alive, He governed His mind by reading the Scriptures of His time—the law of Moses, the prophets, and the psalms or as we know it, the Old Testament. This was his mirror. As a child He was hanging out in the temple and synagogues being "about His father's business." Because Jesus let this become His custom—His daily lifestyle—His mind, will, and emotions were synced up with the limitless God. We are urged to follow His example.

Let this mind be in you, which was also in Christ Jesus: (Phil. 2:5 KJV)

You must have the same attitude that Christ Jesus had. (Phil. 2:5 NLT)

Let is a permissive word, which means you get to decide if you are going to allow what interested and entertained Christ to interest and entertain you. You can permit the same attitudes and opinions that entertained and consumed Christ to entertain and consume you. Or you can decide to let your mind be governed by your mood, emotions, circumstances, or other people rather than by God. The choice is yours.

" 'My Food,' said Jesus, 'is to do the will of him
who sent me and to finish his work.' " (John 4:34 NIV)

"Father, if you are willing, please take this cup of suffering away from me. Yet I want your will to be done, not mine." (Luke 22:42 NLT)

Yes, God loved the world so much that he gave his only Son, so that everyone who believes in him would not be lost but have eternal life. God sent his Son into the world. He did not send him to judge the world guilty, but to save the world through him. (John 3:16-17 ERV)

But the Son of God came to destroy the works of the devil. (1 John 3:8 NLT)

On the sabbath day he went to the synagogue as he always did. He stood up to read. The book of Isaiah the prophet was given to him. He opened the book and found the place where this is written: 'The Spirit of the Lord is on me. He has chosen me to tell good news to the poor. He sent me to tell prisoners that they are free and to tell the blind that they can see again. He sent me to free those who have been treated badly and to announce that the time has come for the Lord to show his kindness. (Luke 4:16b-19 ERV)

Exercises

Exercise 1: Answer the following questions.

1) After reading the Scriptures stated in the Overview of this chapter, how would you describe Christ's mind?

_____
_____
_____
_____
_____
_____

2) Do you currently have the same mind? Circle, yes or no.

3) If yes, how is your mind similar to Jesus' mind? How did you cultivate your mind to be like His?

_____
_____
_____
_____
_____

4) If no, how is your mind different from Jesus' mind? How did you cultivate your mind to be different from His?

_____
_____
_____
_____
_____

5) Are you willing to do what it takes to get and maintain Christ's mind? Yes or no?

6) List some activities, habits, persons, and/or events and describe how they would help you to get and maintain Christ's mind.

_____

_____

_____

_____

_____

_____

_____

_____

_____

_____

_____

_____

_____

_____

_____

_____

_____

_____

_____

_____

_____

_____

_____

_____

Chapter 4: Guard Your Heart

Introduction
In this chapter, you will be asked to assess your relationships. In order to maximize your potential and properly guard your heart and mind, you need to be around the right people.

Overview
> Above all else, guard your heart, for everything you do flows from it. (Prov. 4:23 NIV)

The word **heart** in this verse means your <u>feelings, will, intellect, consent, understanding and mind.</u>

> So we are to keep, guard, protect, or preserve our hearts; the way we think, feel and understand in our minds. And we are to keep watch over what we consent to or give permission to because out of what we think, feel, understand or consent to determine the boundaries or exits of our lives.

The King James Version uses the word 'issues.'

> Keep thy heart with all diligence; for out of it are the issues of life. (Prov. 4:23 KJV)

You may think you have issues but that word **"issues"** means <u>boundaries or exits</u>. You have heard of a glass ceiling in the workplace but it's possible to have a glass ceiling in your heart preventing you from rising to the level God desires for you to be. Eliminating the wrong influences whether they are people or things can help to dispel these ceilings. And surrounding ourselves with the right people and influences will help to propel us forward into a promising future.

> Do not be misled: Bad company corrupts good character. (1 Cor. 15:33 NIV)

Exercises

Exercise 1

1. List the people who are bad company and explain why that is the case. Keep in mind: You may need to list a person that you do not know personally and possibly never met but who is not a good influence on you, such as a singer, actor, or entertainer.

1) _____

_____

_____

2) _____

_____

_____

3) _____
   _____
   _____

4) _____
   _____
   _____

5) _____
   _____
   _____

6) _____
   _____
   _____

7) _____
   _____
   _____

8) _____
   _____
   _____

9) _____
   _____
   _____

10) _____
    _____
    _____

2. What will you do to limit the amount of time you spend with each person? How will you better prepare yourself for interactions with them? An example has been provided to guide you.

Example: For person 1, your answer may be to tell them you need to end the relationship, and you block them from your social media, or unfollow them and block their calls. For person 2, you pray before speaking to them, limit your phone conversations to 15 minutes or less and speak positive affirmations to yourself after you get off of the phone.

Person 1:
_____
_____
_____

Person 2:
_____
_____
_____

Person 3:
_____
_____
_____

Person 4:
_____
_____
_____

Person 5:
_____
_____
_____

Person 6:
_____
_____
_____

Person 7:
_____
_____
_____

Person 8:
_____
_____
_____

Person 9:

_____
_____
_____
_____

Person 10:

_____
_____
_____
_____

3. **Challenge:** Read through your responses in question 2. Identify and list one to three persons that you need to limit time with immediately. Choose to do the actions you listed for that person consistently for the next 30 days. Get an accountability partner who will encourage and support you on your freedom journey.

Person 1: _____

Person 2: _____

Person 3: _____

To Sum It Up

You have taken proper steps in the exercise above to ensure that you limit the amount of exposure you have to people who may distract you from realizing your full potential. While that is a good and very important step, it is not complete all by itself. It's not good enough to clear out the bad. Now that you've made space in your life, make sure you fill it with people who will influence you to move forward in the right direction. I'm confident that you probably already have some people like this in your life. You may need to look a little closer.

Exercise 2

1. List the people who are good company and explain why that is the case. Keep in mind: You may list a person that you do not know personally and possibly may never meet but who is a good influence on you, such as a singer, actor, entertainer, pastor, or motivational speaker.

1) _____
_____
_____

2) _____
   _____
   _____

3) _____
   _____
   _____

4) _____
   _____
   _____

5) _____
   _____
   _____

6) _____
   _____
   _____

7) _____
   _____
   _____

8) _____
   _____
   _____

9) _____
   _____
   _____

10) _____
    _____
    _____

2. How will you strengthen and improve the quality of your relationship with the people you listed?

Person 1:

_____

_____

_____

Person 2:

_____

_____

_____

Person 3:

_____

_____

_____

Person 4:

_____

_____

_____

Person 5:

_____

_____

_____

Person 6:

_____

_____

_____

Person 7:

_____

_____

_____

Person 8:

_____

_____

_____

Person 9:

_____

_____

_____

Person 10:

_____

_____

_____

3. **Challenge:** Read through your responses in question 2. Identify and list one to three persons that you would like to spend more time with. Choose to do the actions you listed for that person consistently for the next 30 days. Get an accountability partner who will encourage and support you on your freedom journey.

Person 1: _____

Person 2: _____

Person 3: _____

Chapter 5: Who Told You That?

Introduction

In this chapter, you will be asked to revisit some unpleasant conversations you have had with others and unpleasant conversations you may have had with yourself. I encourage you to take breaks if you need to and allow yourself to feel whatever emotions arise and think whatever thoughts may come. Going through this may feel painful and difficult at times, I know for me it was. But like the Bible instructs, it's important to guard or to pay attention to our hearts, not to ignore them.

Overview

Words are powerful. Sometimes words can cause pain, insecurities, and rejection issues to surface in our hearts and minds. The old saying, "Sticks and stones may break my bones but words can never hurt me," simply isn't true.

The soothing tongue is a tree of life, but a perverse tongue crushes the spirit. (Prov. 15:4 NIV)

The words of the reckless pierce like swords, (Prov. 12:18-19a NIV)

So also the tongue is a small thing, but what enormous damage it can do. A great forest can be set on fire by one tiny spark. And the tongue is a flame of fire. It is full of wickedness, and poisons every part of the body. And the tongue is set on fire by hell itself and can turn our whole lives into a blazing flame of destruction and disaster. (James 3:5-6 TLB)

Many of the **Either/Or** thoughts people contend with were derived from words spoken over them by others. And in some cases, people have spoken damaging words over themselves.

Ask yourself the following:

Who told you ...
- "You're not smart enough."
- "You're not pretty enough."
- "You're not strong enough."
- "You're not rich enough."
- "You're too young."
- "You're too old."
- "You're too dark."
- "You're too light."
- "You're too fat."
- "You're too skinny."
- "Women can't do that."
- "Men don't do that."
- "Your past has disqualified you."

Exercises

Exercise 1: In the space provided write the names of people, not including yourself, who you remember saying anything unpleasant or hurtful to you. If you do not know the name or do not remember the name, make up a name or describe the person.

Write the name of each person and write the statement that he or she said.

1) Name: _____
   Statement: _____
   _____

2) Name: _____
   Statement: _____
   _____

3) Name: _____
   Statement: _____
   _____

4) Name: _____
   Statement: _____
   _____

5) Name: _____
   Statement: _____
   _____

6) Name: _____
   Statement: _____
   _____

7) Name: _____
   Statement: _____
   _____

8) Name: _____
   Statement: _____
   _____

9) Name: _____
   Statement: _____

10) Name: _____

    Statement: _____

    _____

11) Name: _____

    Statement: _____

    _____

12) Name: _____

    Statement: _____

    _____

13) Name: _____

    Statement: _____

    _____

14) Name: _____

    Statement: _____

    _____

15) Name: _____

    Statement: _____

16) Name: _____

    Statement: _____

    _____

17) Name: _____

    Statement: _____

    _____

    _____

18) Name: _____

    Statement: _____

    _____

19) Name: _____

    Statement: _____

    _____

20) Name: _____

    Statement: _____

    _____

Exercise 2: Write down how these statements made or make you feel. What thoughts immediately come to mind concerning yourself and/or others when you read the statements?

Statement 1:_____

_____

_____

Statement 2:_____

_____

_____

Statement 3:_____

_____

_____

Statement 4:_____

_____

_____

Statement 5:_____

_____

_____

Statement 6:_____

_____

_____

Statement 7:_____

_____

_____

Statement 8:_____

_____

_____

Statement 9:_____

_____

_____

Statement 10:_____

_____

_____

Statement 12:_____

_____

Statement 13:_____
_____
_____

Statement14:_____
_____
_____

Statement 15:_____
_____
_____

Statement 16:_____
_____
_____

Statement 17:_____
_____
_____

Statement 18:_____
_____
_____

Statement 19:_____
_____
_____

Statement 20:_____
_____
_____

Exercise 3: Answer the following questions.

1) Do you agree with the statement the person made? Circle, yes or no, and then explain, why or why not.

Statement 1: Yes or No Explain:_____
_____
_____

Statement 2: Yes or No Explain:_____
_____
_____

Statement 3: Yes or No Explain: _____
_____
_____

Statement 4: Yes or No Explain: _____
_____
_____

Statement 5: Yes or No Explain: _____
_____
_____

Statement 6: Yes or No Explain: _____
_____
_____

Statement 7: Yes or No Explain: _____
_____
_____

Statement 8: Yes or No Explain: _____
_____
_____

Statement 9: Yes or No Explain: _____
_____
_____

Statement 10: Yes or No Explain: _____
_____
_____

Statement 11: Yes or No Explain: _____
_____
_____

Statement 12: Yes or No Explain: _____
_____
_____

Statement 13: Yes or No Explain: _____
_____
_____

Statement 14: Yes or No Explain: _____
_____
_____

Statement 15: Yes or No Explain: _____
_____
_____

Statement 16: Yes or No Explain: _____
_____
_____

Statement 17: Yes or No Explain: _____
_____
_____

Statement 18: Yes or No Explain: _____
_____
_____

Statement 19: Yes or No Explain: _____
_____
_____

Statement 20: Yes or No Explain: _____
_____
_____

2) How have these statements impacted you?

_____
_____
_____
_____
_____
_____
_____
_____
_____
_____
_____
_____
_____
_____
_____
_____
_____
_____
_____
_____
_____

_____

_____

_____

_____

_____

_____

_____

_____

_____

_____

_____

_____

_____

_____

Exercise 4: Answer the following questions:

What negative statements have you or do you say to yourself?

List the statements and answer the subsequent questions.

Statement 1: _____

When do you say it? _____

_____

_____

_____

Why do you say it? _____

_____

_____

_____

How does it affect your mood? _____

_____

_____

_____

How does it affect how you view and relate to others? _____

_____

_____

_____

How does it affect how you view and treat yourself? _____

_____

_____

_____

How does it affect your actions, reactions, and decision-making process? _____
_____
_____
_____

Statement 2: _____

When do you say it? _____
_____
_____
_____

Why do you say it? _____
_____
_____
_____

How does it affect your mood? _____
_____
_____

How does it affect how you view and relate to others? _____
_____
_____
_____

How does it affect how you view and treat yourself? _____
_____
_____
_____

How does it affect your actions, reactions, and decision-making process? _____
_____
_____
_____

Statement 3: _____

When do you say it? _____
_____
_____
_____

Why do you say it? _____
_____
_____

How does it affect your mood? _____
_____
_____
_____

How does it affect how you view and relate to others? _____
_____
_____
_____

How does it affect how you view and treat yourself? _____
_____
_____
_____

How does it affect your actions, reactions, and decision-making process? _____
_____
_____
_____

Statement 4: _____
When do you say it? _____
_____
_____
_____

Why do you say it? _____
_____
_____
_____

How does it affect your mood? _____
_____
_____
_____

How does it affect how you view and relate to others? _____
_____
_____
_____

How does it affect how you view and treat yourself? _____
_____
_____
_____

How does it affect your actions, reactions, and decision-making process? _____
_____
_____
_____

Statement 5: _____

When do you say it? _____
_____
_____
_____

Why do you say it? _____
_____
_____
_____

How does it affect your mood? _____
_____
_____
_____

How does it affect how you view and relate to others? _____
_____
_____
_____

How does it affect how you view and treat yourself? _____
_____
_____
_____

How does it affect your actions, reactions, and decision-making process? _____
_____
_____
_____

Statement 6: _____

When do you say it? _____
_____
_____
_____

Why do you say it? _____
_____
_____
_____

How does it affect your mood? _____
_____
_____
_____

How does it affect how you view and relate to others? _____
_____
_____
_____

How does it affect how you view and treat yourself? _____
_____
_____
_____

How does it affect your actions, reactions, and decision-making process? _____
_____
_____
_____

Statement 7: _____

When do you say it? _____
_____
_____
_____

Why do you say it? _____
_____
_____
_____

How does it affect your mood? _____
_____
_____
_____

How does it affect how you view and relate to others? _____
_____
_____
_____

How does it affect how you view and treat yourself? _____
_____
_____
_____

How does it affect your actions, reactions, and decision-making process? _____
_____
_____
_____

Statement 8: _____

When do you say it? _____
_____
_____
_____

Why do you say it? _____
_____
_____
_____

How does it affect your mood? _____
_____
_____
_____

How does it affect how you view and relate to others? _____
_____
_____
_____

How does it affect how you view and treat yourself? _____
_____
_____
_____

How does it affect your actions, reactions, and decision-making process? _____
_____
_____
_____

Statement 9: _____

When do you say it? _____
_____
_____

Why do you say it? _____

_____

_____

_____

How does it affect your mood? _____

_____

_____

_____

How does it affect how you view and relate to others? _____

_____

_____

_____

How does it affect how you view and treat yourself? _____

_____

_____

_____

How does it affect your actions, reactions, and decision-making process? _____

_____

_____

_____

Statement 10: _____

When do you say it? _____

_____

_____

_____

Why do you say it? _____

_____

_____

_____

How does it affect your mood? _____

_____

_____

_____

How does it affect how you view and relate to others? _____
_____
_____
_____

How does it affect how you view and treat yourself? _____
_____
_____
_____

How does it affect your actions, reactions, and decision-making process? _____
_____
_____
_____

To Sum It Up

One thing to remember about self-hatred is that it is never the will of God. He loves you even if you don't love yourself. If you choose to embrace His love for you, then you will learn how to love yourself as well. I am not just talking theory; I'm telling you what I know. Suicidal tendencies and depression used to be my best friends but not anymore. God's love is a mighty weapon, and it wants to work for you today. In chapters 9-11 you will go through exercises that will assist you in speaking words of life over yourself.

Chapter 6: What Happened To You?

Introduction

In the following exercises you will be asked to identify some life-altering events that may have scarred you spiritually, mentally, emotionally, and physically. Although this may be painful, please answer truthfully as your freedom is connected to sorting through these events and the emotions and thoughts that may have come as a result.

Overview

What happened to you?

- Perhaps you were abandoned as a child.
- Maybe you had an abortion and are struggling to forgive yourself.
- Maybe you committed a crime and have to deal with the consequences of that decision daily.
- Maybe you were molested, raped, or sexually assaulted.
- Maybe you suffered a divorce.
- Maybe someone you loved died.
- Maybe something else happened I did not list.

When life-altering events happen, it can leave us feeling disappointed, resentful, victimized, hopeless, scared, saddened, and angry. As frustrating as it may be, neither you nor I can change the unfortunate situations that happened to us. It already happened. No matter how badly we may want to rewrite history, it is impossible. But while it is impossible to change the past, we do have the power to prevent the past from causing despair in our present and future.

Exercises

Exercise 1: In the space provided, list what happened.

Offense 1: _____

Offense 2: _____

Offense 3: _____

Offense 4: _____

Offense 5: _____

Offense 6: _____

Offense 7: _____

Offense 8: _____

Offense 9: _____

Offense 10: _____

Offense 11: _____

Offense 12: _____

Offense 13: _____

Offense 14: _____

Offense 15: _____

Offense 16: _____

Offense 17: _____

Offense 18: _____

Offense 19: _____

Offense 20: _____

Exercise 2: Answer the following questions:

1) Do you believe you have some **Either/Or** thoughts that were created as a direct result of one or more of the offenses listed in Exercise 1? Circle: Yes or No.

2) If yes, list the offense below and the **Either/Or** thought that resulted.

Offense 1: _____
I can **Either** _____
Or _____

Offense 2: _____
I can **Either** _____
Or _____

Offense 3: _____
I can **Either** _____
Or _____

Offense 4: _____
I can **Either** _____
Or _____

Offense 5: _____
I can **Either** _____

Or _____

Offense 6: _____
I can **Either** _____
Or _____

Offense 7: _____
I can **Either** _____
Or _____

Offense 8: _____
I can **Either** _____
Or _____

Offense 9: _____
I can **Either** _____
Or _____

Offense 10: _____
I can **Either** _____
Or _____

Offense 11: _____
I can **Either** _____
Or _____

Offense 12: _____
I can **Either** _____
Or _____

Offense 13: _____
I can **Either** _____
Or _____

Offense 14: _____
I can **Either** _____
Or _____

Offense 15: _____
I can **Either** _____
Or _____

Offense 16: _____
I can **Either** _____
Or _____

Offense 17: _____
I can **Either** _____
Or _____

Offense 18: _____
I can **Either** _____
Or _____
Offense 19: _____
I can **Either** _____
Or _____

Offense 20: _____
I can **Either** _____
Or _____

> **When we become offended, we get trapped internally in a scandal and are more susceptible to falling away from our relationship with God and identity in Jesus Christ.**

I am sorry that you have suffered these offenses. But unfortunately, you may become offended even more in the future. Even Jesus told us that offenses will come (Matt. 18:7 KJV). The problem with this is that according to Strong's Concordance Dictionary, the word **offenses** in this verse means scandal, trap, and occasion to fall.

The key to freedom from these offenses is forgiveness. God does not want us to live in offense. So, God through Jesus Christ gives us the power to forgive.

Chapter 7: How To Choose To Forgive

The exercises in this chapter are designed to help you walk through the process of forgiveness. I use the term process because it may not be fully completed the first time you go through the exercises. In fact, you may have to repeat them over and over again. No harm done. Be patient with yourself and choose to enjoy and benefit from the process. And choose not to compare your process to someone else's.

Overview

Satan is the enemy of our soul, and unfortunately, he influences other people to hurt us. Even if the person he used to offend us was our grandparent, parent, sibling, neighbor, teacher, co-worker, spouse, or friend, the source was Satan.

Our fight is not against people on earth. We are fighting against the rulers and authorities and the powers of this world's darkness. We are fighting against the rulers and authorities and the powers of evil in heavenly places. (Eph. 6:12 ERV)

If we don't recognize this, we could spend a lifetime angry and bitter toward the people he influenced to say those rotten things to us. Then, unforgiveness gets into our hearts and can potentially cause emotional and spiritual heart failure. None of us can afford to embrace unforgiveness.

If you forgive those who sin against you, your heavenly Father will forgive you. But if you refuse to forgive others, your Father will not forgive your sins. (Matt. 6:14-15 NLT)

You may have experienced some traumatic circumstances that have left wounds in your soul. I am not suggesting that you ignore those wounds but acknowledge them. If you recognize those wounds, then you can heal and successfully move past them. And I passionately believe that you deserve that. The only way this can happen is if you forgive those who have done you harm.

The word **forgive** in the Hebrew and Greek Strong's Concordance Dictionary usually means to "send away." We need to actively send away those negative emotions attached to those painful memories of what happened to us or did not happen for us in our past. When we realize who our real enemy is, we can release those people who hurt us and not allow their error to paralyze our present or dictate our future. Instead, we can press aggressively forward into what God has for us.

Confront, Don't Deny

Sometimes we are upset with someone and we have never communicated our discontented feelings with them. Unfortunately, it is not always possible to open up and share our feelings with the person who offended us. The person may be deceased or may have been a stranger. If this is the case you may have to use your imagination. You may need to visualize them sitting in a chair and communicate your offense. You may need to write them a letter you never mail. Whatever you need to do … do it.

But if you can speak with the person, I recommend that you do. They may not respond the way you would have liked but at least you will be following God's scriptural directions for reconciliation.

If your brother or sister in God's family does something wrong, go and tell them what they did wrong. Do this when you are alone with them. If they listen to you, then you have helped them to be your brother or sister again. (Matt. 18:15 ERV)

Exercise 1:

a) Think about who you need to speak to one-on-one concerning an offense and use the lines below to write out what you will say.

b) Pray about and write down how and when you plan to have this conversation. More space is provided in the back of the workbook.

_____
_____
_____
_____
_____
_____
_____
_____
_____
_____
_____
_____
_____
_____

Forgiveness is not for the other person. It is for you. It is a gift you give yourself.

_____
_____
_____
_____
_____
_____
_____
_____
_____
_____
_____
_____
_____
_____
_____
_____

_____

_____

_____

_____

_____

_____

_____

_____

_____

The pain might not be your fault but the healing is your responsibility.

Kimberly Jones-Pothier

When it comes to our emotional, internal, and spiritual healing, we are in the driver's seat. It's easy to blame others and circumstances for the things we do not like, but this will not foster and effect change.

This may be tough to hear but it is true. Many of us expect God to heal us and wait for years for Him to do it. But the reality is, Jesus already did on the cross when He chose to die and said, "It is finished." Now it is up to us to stay healed— emotionally, physically, mentally, and spiritually.

We maintain our internal peace, the peace Jesus died to give us, by controlling our minds and fixing them on the right things (John 14:27). And we have the grace to do this no matter what we've been through or might be going through right now.

You will keep in perfect peace all who trust in you,
all whose thoughts are fixed on you! (Isa. 26:3 NLT)

Do you want perfect—mature and complete—peace with nothing missing or broken? It is yours if you keep your mind fixed on Jesus and not on the abuse or abuser. Whatever you meditate on, gets bigger. Meditate on the problem and it will grow. Meditate on the solution and that will grow.

God loves you! His love for you does not diminish because another person didn't value you enough to love you the same. Perhaps something terrible did happen to you. Maybe it's so traumatic that you could say you suffered an internal death. But that does not have to be the end of your story. No matter what violations you have suffered, none of them are strong enough to destroy your life in Christ Jesus without your permission. Be relentless in your pursuit of greatness regardless of what you may have suffered.

Exercises

Exercise 2: Fill in the blanks beginning with the name of the person who offended you. Once you have filled in the blanks, read the statement aloud. You can reference your exercise responses about offenses from Chapter 6 to help you complete the statements.

1) (Name) _____, I forgive you for _____
   _____
   _____.
   I send the pain, offense, bitterness, resentment, shame, embarrassment, and regret away. I cast this care upon Jesus, because I know He cares for me.

2) (Name) _____, I forgive you for _____
   _____
   _____.
   I send the pain, offense, bitterness, resentment, shame, embarrassment, and regret away. I cast this care upon Jesus, because I know He cares for me.

3) (Name) _____, I forgive you for _____
   _____
   _____.
   I send the pain, offense, bitterness, resentment, shame, embarrassment, and regret away. I cast this care upon Jesus, because I know He cares for me.

4) (Name) _____, I forgive you for _____
   _____
   _____.
   I send the pain, offense, bitterness, resentment, shame, embarrassment, and regret away. I cast this care upon Jesus, because I know He cares for me.

5) (Name) _____, I forgive you for _____
   _____
   _____.
   I send the pain, offense, bitterness, resentment, shame, embarrassment, and regret away. I cast this care upon Jesus, because I know He cares for me.

6) (Name) _____, I forgive you for _____
   _____
   _____.
   I send the pain, offense, bitterness, resentment, shame, embarrassment, and regret away. I cast this care upon Jesus, because I know He cares for me.

7) (Name) _____, I forgive you for _____
_____
_____.
I send the pain, offense, bitterness, resentment, shame, embarrassment, and regret away. I cast this care upon Jesus, because I know He cares for me.

8) (Name) _____, I forgive you for _____
_____
_____.
I send the pain, offense, bitterness, resentment, shame, embarrassment, and regret away. I cast this care upon Jesus, because I know He cares for me.

9) (Name) _____, I forgive you for _____
_____
_____.
I send the pain, offense, bitterness, resentment, shame, embarrassment, and regret away. I cast this care upon Jesus, because I know He cares for me.

10) (Name) _____, I forgive you for _____
_____
_____.
I send the pain, offense, bitterness, resentment, shame, embarrassment, and regret away. I cast this care upon Jesus, because I know He cares for me.

11) (Name) _____, I forgive you for _____
_____
_____.
I send the pain, offense, bitterness, resentment, shame, embarrassment, and regret away. I cast this care upon Jesus, because I know He cares for me.

12) (Name) _____, I forgive you for _____
_____
_____.
I send the pain, offense, bitterness, resentment, shame, embarrassment, and regret away. I cast this care upon Jesus, because I know He cares for me.

13) (Name) _____, I forgive you for _____
_____
_____.
I send the pain, offense, bitterness, resentment, shame, embarrassment, and regret away. I cast this care upon Jesus, because I know He cares for me.

14) (Name) _____, I forgive you for _____
_____.
I send the pain, offense, bitterness, resentment, shame, embarrassment, and regret away. I cast this care upon Jesus, because I know He cares for me.

15) (Name) _____, I forgive you for _____

_____

_____.
I send the pain, offense, bitterness, resentment, shame, embarrassment, and regret away. I cast this care upon Jesus, because I know He cares for me.

16) (Name) _____, I forgive you for _____

_____

_____.
I send the pain, offense, bitterness, resentment, shame, embarrassment, and regret away. I cast this care upon Jesus, because I know He cares for me.

17) (Name) _____, I forgive you for _____

_____

_____.
I send the pain, offense, bitterness, resentment, shame, embarrassment, and regret away. I cast this care upon Jesus, because I know He cares for me.

18) (Name) _____, I forgive you for _____

_____

_____.
I send the pain, offense, bitterness, resentment, shame, embarrassment, and regret away. I cast this care upon Jesus, because I know He cares for me.

19) (Name) _____, I forgive you for _____

_____

_____.
I send the pain, offense, bitterness, resentment, shame, embarrassment, and regret away. I cast this care upon Jesus, because I know He cares for me.

20) (Name) _____, I forgive you for _____

_____

_____.
I send the pain, offense, bitterness, resentment, shame, embarrassment, and regret away. I cast this care upon Jesus, because I know He cares for me.

Give all your worries and cares to God, for he cares about you. (1 Pet. 5:7 NLT)

Exercise 3: Speak well of the person. In Matthew 5, Jesus told us how to love our enemies. He instructed us to "pray for them which despitefully use you, and persecute you." Insert the same names you listed from Exercise 2 into the prayer below. There is added space if you feel led to pray your own words.

1) (Name) _____, I pray God's best over your life. I pray that you are healthy, wealthy, and wise. I pray that you will not hurt anyone else and that any pain you are or have experienced yourself will be washed away in the blood of Jesus.

_____

_____

_____.

2) (Name) _____, I pray God's best over your life. I pray that you are healthy, wealthy, and wise. I pray that you will not hurt anyone else and that any pain you are or have experienced yourself will be washed away in the blood of Jesus.

_____

_____

_____.

3) (Name) _____, I pray God's best over your life. I pray that you are healthy, wealthy, and wise. I pray that you will not hurt anyone else and that any pain you are or have experienced yourself will be washed away in the blood of Jesus.

_____

_____

_____.

4) (Name) _____, I pray God's best over your life. I pray that you are healthy, wealthy, and wise. I pray that you will not hurt anyone else and that any pain you are or have experienced yourself will be washed away in the blood of Jesus.

_____

_____

_____.

5) (Name) _____, I pray God's best over your life. I pray that you are healthy, wealthy, and wise. I pray that you will not hurt anyone else and that any pain you are or have experienced yourself will be washed away in the blood of Jesus.

_____

_____

_____

6) (Name) _____, I pray God's best over your life. I pray that you are healthy, wealthy, and wise. I pray that you will not hurt anyone else and that any pain you are or have experienced yourself will be washed away in the blood of Jesus.

_____
_____
_____.

7) (Name) _____, I pray God's best over your life. I pray that you are healthy, wealthy, and wise. I pray that you will not hurt anyone else and that any pain you are or have experienced yourself will be washed away in the blood of Jesus.

_____
_____
_____.

8) (Name) _____, I pray God's best over your life. I pray that you are healthy, wealthy, and wise. I pray that you will not hurt anyone else and that any pain you are or have experienced yourself will be washed away in the blood of Jesus.

_____
_____
_____.

9) (Name) _____, I pray God's best over your life. I pray that you are healthy, wealthy, and wise. I pray that you will not hurt anyone else and that any pain you are or have experienced yourself will be washed away in the blood of Jesus.

_____
_____
_____.

10) (Name) _____, I pray God's best over your life. I pray that you are healthy, wealthy, and wise. I pray that you will not hurt anyone else and that any pain you are or have experienced yourself will be washed away in the blood of Jesus.

_____
_____
_____.

11) (Name) _____, I pray God's best over your life. I pray that you are healthy, wealthy, and wise. I pray that you will not hurt anyone else and that any pain you are or have experienced yourself will be washed away in the blood of Jesus.

_____
_____
_____.

12) (Name) _____, I pray God's best over your life. I pray that you are healthy, wealthy, and wise. I pray that you will not hurt anyone else and that any pain you are or have experienced yourself will be washed away in the blood of Jesus.

_____
_____
_____.

13) (Name) _____, I pray God's best over your life. I pray that you are healthy, wealthy, and wise. I pray that you will not hurt anyone else and that any pain you are or have experienced yourself will be washed away in the blood of Jesus.

_____
_____
_____.

14) (Name) _____, I pray God's best over your life. I pray that you are healthy, wealthy, and wise. I pray that you will not hurt anyone else and that any pain you are or have experienced yourself will be washed away in the blood of Jesus.

_____
_____
_____.

15) (Name) _____, I pray God's best over your life. I pray that you are healthy, wealthy, and wise. I pray that you will not hurt anyone else and that any pain you are or have experienced yourself will be washed away in the blood of Jesus.

_____
_____
_____.

16) (Name) _____, I pray God's best over your life. I pray that you are healthy, wealthy, and wise. I pray that you will not hurt anyone else and that any pain you are or have experienced yourself will be washed away in the blood of Jesus.

_____
_____
_____.

17) (Name) _____, I pray God's best over your life. I pray that you are healthy, wealthy, and wise. I pray that you will not hurt anyone else and that any pain you are or have experienced yourself will be washed away in the blood of Jesus.

_____
_____
_____.

18) (Name) _____, I pray God's best over your life. I pray that you are healthy, wealthy, and wise. I pray that you will not hurt anyone else and that any pain you are or have experienced yourself will be washed away in the blood of Jesus.

_____

_____

_____.

19) (Name) _____, I pray God's best over your life. I pray that you are healthy, wealthy, and wise. I pray that you will not hurt anyone else and that any pain you are or have experienced yourself will be washed away in the blood of Jesus.

_____

_____

_____.

20) (Name) _____, I pray God's best over your life. I pray that you are healthy, wealthy, and wise. I pray that you will not hurt anyone else and that any pain you are or have experienced yourself will be washed away in the blood of Jesus.

_____

_____

_____.

Bonus: Use the lines below to write a personalized prayer for someone or everyone you listed above.

_____

_____

_____

_____

_____

_____

_____

_____

_____

_____

_____

_____

_____

Exercise 4: In some cases, hurtful circumstances were not our fault, and we did not play a part in what happened to us. However, in some situations, we are responsible for causing harm. For those times, we need to forgive ourselves. And all of us may need to forgive ourselves for harboring unforgiveness in our hearts. If the person you need to forgive is yourself, write your name and the offense you committed on the spaces provided.

1) I, _____, forgive myself for _____
_____
_____.
I send the pain, offence, bitterness, resentment, shame, embarrassment and regret away. I pray God's best over my life. I declare that I am healthy, wealthy and wise. I will not hurt anyone else by God's grace and the pain I have experienced is washed away in the blood of Jesus.

2) I, _____, forgive myself for _____
_____
_____.
I send the pain, offence, bitterness, resentment, shame, embarrassment and regret away. I pray God's best over my life. I declare that I am healthy, wealthy and wise. I will not hurt anyone else by God's grace and the pain I have experienced is washed away in the blood of Jesus.

3) I, _____, forgive myself for _____
_____
_____.
I send the pain, offence, bitterness, resentment, shame, embarrassment and regret away. I pray God's best over my life. I declare that I am healthy, wealthy and wise. I will not hurt anyone else by God's grace and the pain I have experienced is washed away in the blood of Jesus.

4) I, _____, forgive myself for _____
_____
_____.
I send the pain, offence, bitterness, resentment, shame, embarrassment and regret away. I pray God's best over my life. I declare that I am healthy, wealthy and wise. I will not hurt anyone else by God's grace and the pain I have experienced is washed away in the blood of Jesus.

5) I, _____, forgive myself for _____
_____
_____.
I send the pain, offence, bitterness, resentment, shame, embarrassment and regret away. I pray God's best over my life. I declare that I am healthy, wealthy and wise. I will not hurt anyone else by God's grace and the pain I have experienced is washed away in the blood of Jesus.

6) I, _____, forgive myself for _____
_____
_____.
I send the pain, offence, bitterness, resentment, shame, embarrassment and regret away. I pray God's best over my life. I declare that I am healthy, wealthy and wise. I will not hurt anyone else by God's grace and the pain I have experienced is washed away in the blood of Jesus.

7) I, _____, forgive myself for _____
_____
_____.

I send the pain, offence, bitterness, resentment, shame, embarrassment and regret away. I pray God's best over my life. I declare that I am healthy, wealthy and wise. I will not hurt anyone else by God's grace and the pain I have experienced is washed away in the blood of Jesus.

8) I, _____, forgive myself for _____
_____
_____.

I send the pain, offence, bitterness, resentment, shame, embarrassment and regret away. I pray God's best over my life. I declare that I am healthy, wealthy and wise. I will not hurt anyone else by God's grace and the pain I have experienced is washed away in the blood of Jesus.

9) I, _____, forgive myself for _____
_____
_____.

I send the pain, offence, bitterness, resentment, shame, embarrassment and regret away. I pray God's best over my life. I declare that I am healthy, wealthy and wise. I will not hurt anyone else by God's grace and the pain I have experienced is washed away in the blood of Jesus.

10) I, _____, forgive myself for _____
_____
_____.

I send the pain, offence, bitterness, resentment, shame, embarrassment and regret away. I pray God's best over my life. I declare that I am healthy, wealthy and wise. I will not hurt anyone else by God's grace and the pain I have experienced is washed away in the blood of Jesus.

Exercise 5: Speak well of yourself. If you have been an enemy to yourself, then Jesus instructs you to show love to yourself and pray for yourself. Please complete the declaration below.

I, _____, speak well over myself. I am _____
_____
_____
_____
_____
_____
_____
_____
_____.

Many of us try to heal apart from others, but I don't believe this is possible. I am an introvert and was raised primarily by a single parent and was an only child up until I was 14 so this is difficult for me. I would much rather pray alone, write in my journal, and pour my heart out to God. But while that may help me to feel better for a time, it is not the complete model God created for restoration. He never intended for us to be islands unto ourselves.

Make this your common practice: Confess your sins to each other and pray for each other so that you can live together whole

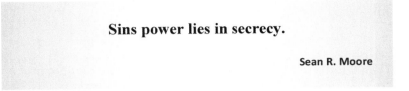

Sins power lies in secrecy.

Sean R. Moore

and healed. The prayer of a person living right with God is something powerful to be reckoned with.

(James 5:16 MSG)

We are a part of the Body of Christ, not the Individual of Christ. I know it can be really intimidating to admit your flaws to someone else. And sometimes it's easier to live with a mask on than to face our true identity with all of our mistakes. Sharing them with someone else can make us feel vulnerable. But when we choose the right person who has our best interest at heart and will allow God to use them to bless us, our lives will be greatly enhanced. Allow your sister or brother in Christ to pray for you so that you can be completely healed.

Once you expose the shame, you have no reason to be ashamed anymore.

Exercise 6:

List the names of the people you can share certain personal faults with and commit to a date to tell them by.

1) _____ Date: _____
2) _____ Date: _____
3) _____ Date: _____
4) _____ Date: _____
5) _____ Date: _____

In this chapter, I have walked you through action steps you can take to help rid yourself of unforgivness toward yourself and others. But what if the One you are really angry with is God? I have been angry with God many times. Like when my mom died. I didn't and still don't fully understand why, how, what went wrong, and why we couldn't fix it. Maybe you have been angry, disappointed, or saddened by what seemed like indifference or neglect or even abandonment from God. Have you ever thought, "Where was God when this happened? Why didn't he warn me? Why won't He do something?" If you have, join the club. While it is unlikely for many Christians to admit it, many of us have or are at this time at least a tad bit offended by God. And this could trap us in a state of spiritual stagnation, thus affecting other areas of our lives if we don't do something about it. Take a moment to search your heart with the following exercises.

Exercise 7: List personal experiences or world events that have occurred that caused you to question God's love and/or goodness.

1) _____

2) _____

3) _____

4) _____

5) _____

6) _____

Don't throw away what you do know for what you don't know.

Bob Yandian

7) _____

8) _____

9) _____

10) _____

In life, you won't be able to explain everything. Don't fall into the trap of rejecting what you do know to be true about God, life, you and the world around you just because some things are unexplainable.

Exercise 8: Complete the following in the space provided below.
   a) Now, talk to God about each thing listed above in Exercise 7 and be honest. Tell Him how you felt then and how you feel now.
   b) Ask Him any question you want.
   c) Jot down the responses He gives.

Remember: The same things you did for yourself and others in the previous exercises to forgive them, you must do for God. Speak well of Him and remind yourself of His character as described in Scripture. This is the truth even if your experience seems to suggest otherwise.

Note: As you begin to complete this exercise, you might not get the answers you want immediately, but remember, you are His sheep, and He is a good Shepherd. You can hear His voice, and He will lead you the way you should go no matter what (Ps. 23, John 10:27).

_____
_____
_____
_____
_____
_____
_____
_____
_____
_____
_____
_____
_____
_____
_____
_____
_____
_____
_____
_____
_____
_____
_____
_____
_____
_____
_____
_____
_____
_____
_____
_____
_____
_____
_____
_____
_____

Chapter 8: But What If My Circumstances Don't Change?

Introduction

In this chapter, you will be asked to evaluate your mindset concerning fulfillment. You need to ask yourself the question, "What am I waiting for?

> **Whenever you can't change what's happening around you, work to change what's going on within you.**

Overview

Many people think that in order to truly be happy, full of peace, and go after their dreams, they have to wait until their circumstances become more favorable. They have to wait until they get a new job, a new house, a divorce, get married, have a baby, or send their child to college, etc. But when Jesus died on the cross, He said, "It is finished!" (John 19:30). It – whatever you are looking forward to — has already been provided for by His sacrifice.

He that spared not his own Son, but delivered Him over for us all, how will He not also with Him freely give us all things? (Rom. 8:32)

Throughout the previous chapters, we have seen how various experiences may not have turned out the way we expected. When that happens, sometimes it could feel like our dreams and goals have failed or even died. Even the disciples were shocked when Jesus died, thinking that their devotion to Him was in vain. Although it may seem this way, I want to encourage you to hold on. And just like the disciples, you will see the resurrection of your dead dream. Sometimes, God gives us a new dream. Open your heart to His goodness for your life.

Exercises

Exercise 1: List all of the dreams you are looking forward to in life.

I am looking forward to:

1) _____

_____

2) _____

_____

3) _____

_____

4) _____
_____

5) _____
_____

6) _____
_____

7) _____
_____

8) _____
_____

9) _____
_____

10) _____
_____

11) _____
_____

12) _____
_____

13) _____
_____

14) _____
_____

15) _____
_____

16) _____
_____

17) _____
_____

18) _____
_____

19) _____
_____

20) _____
_____

Exercise 2:

a) In reviewing the things you wrote down in the previous exercise, what dreams are you waiting for with the thinking that, "Until I get to this point, I won't truly be fulfilled or happy?" Be honest. List them on the lines provided below.

b) Then, in the space provided place a checkmark if you believe that dream can and will happen for you. Again, be honest.

1) [___] _____
_____

2) [___] _____
_____

3) [___] _____
_____

4) [___] _____
_____

5) [___] _____
_____

6) [___] _____
_____

7) [___] _____
_____

8) [___] _____
_____

9) [___] _____
_____

10)[___] _____
_____

11) [＿] _____
   _____

12) [＿] _____
   _____

13) [＿] _____
   _____

14) [＿] _____
   _____

15) [＿] _____
   _____

16) [＿] _____
   _____

17) [＿] _____
   _____

18) [＿] _____
   _____

19) [＿] _____
   _____

20) [＿] _____
   _____

Exercise 3: Create a list of steps to complete within the next 30 days to help you achieve at least one of the dreams you listed in Exercise 3. More space is provided in the back of the workbook.

Dream: _____
Steps: _____
_____
_____
_____
_____

Dream: _____

Steps: _____

_____

_____

_____

_____

Dream: _____

Steps: _____

_____

_____

_____

_____

Dream: _____

Steps: _____

_____

_____

_____

_____

Dream: _____

Steps: _____

_____

_____

_____

_____

Exercise 4: Review your responses to Exercise 2. If there were some dreams that you did not place a checkmark by, use the lines below to explain why you do not believe these dreams will manifest.

_____

_____

_____

_____

_____

_____

_____

Exercise 5: If you completed Exercise 4 because you were unable to complete exercises 2 and 3, then go back to Chapter 4 and revisit your responses. Also, review Chapter 6 and forgive those you need to forgive.

Exercise 6: Answer the following questions.

1) If the dreams you listed in Exercise 1 do not happen or do not happen how you think they should, how will you respond to ensure you are still content?

_____
_____
_____
_____
_____

2) If you never move away from the environment or person(s) causing you pain, what will you do to ensure you will still be happy?

_____
_____
_____
_____
_____

3) Do you believe it's possible to be happy if the unfortunate circumstances in your life don't change? Circle, yes or no.

Explain:_____
_____
_____
_____
_____

4) What 5 things can you do within the next 30 days to assist you with your happiness even in the midst of unchanging circumstances?

_____
_____
_____
_____
_____

Isaiah said, "You will keep in perfect peace all who trust in you, all whose thoughts are fixed on you!"
(Isa. 26:3 NLT)

Jesus said, "I am leaving you with a gift – peace of mind and heart. And the peace I give is a gift the world cannot give. So don't be troubled or afraid."
(John 14:27 NLT)

Chapter 9: What Does The Word Say?

Introduction
In this chapter, you will begin to combat and subdue your **Either/Or** thoughts with Scriptures from the Bible.

Overview

Paul said, "Not that I was ever in need, for I have learned how to get along happily whether I have much or little. I know how to live on almost nothing or with everything. I have learned the secret of contentment in every situation, whether it be a full stomach or hunger, plenty or want." (Phil. 4:11-12 TLB)

> **Whenever you can't change what's happening around you, work to change what's going on within you.**

I believe that like Paul, we can learn how to be content no matter what we are going through. I am reminded of an extremely tough time in my life. One in which I had given up hope that circumstances would change for the better. It was difficult to be optimistic, let alone be in faith. I dreaded waking up in the morning and suicide seemed like a more viable option—the only thing that could permanently change my circumstances. Or so I thought. I have been on this internal ledge on more than one occasion spanning various years resulting from a degree of varying circumstances. But one day I decided that regardless of how much I wanted my situations to change and felt powerless to change them, I would begin to work on changing how I perceived them.

And now, dear brothers and sisters, one final thing. Fix your thoughts on what is true, and honorable, and right, and pure, and lovely, and admirable. Think about things that are excellent and worthy of praise. (Phil. 4:8 NLT)

Exercises

Exercise 1: List everything going on in your life right now that is true, honorable, right, pure, lovely, admirable, excellent, and praiseworthy.

1) _____

_____

2) _____

_____

3) _____

_____

4) _____

_____

5) _____

_____

6) _____

_____

7) _____

_____

8) _____

_____

9) _____

_____

10) _____

_____

11) _____

_____

12) _____

_____

13) _____

_____

14) _____

_____

15) _____

_____

16) _____

_____

17) _____

_____

18) _____

_____

19) _____

_____

20) _____

_____

To all who mourn in Israel he will give: beauty for ashes; joy instead of mourning; praise instead of heaviness. For God has planted them like strong and graceful oaks for his own glory. (Isa. 61:3)

Gratitude and thankfulness are the antidotes I
embrace to combat depression.

Exercise 2: Take a moment to thank God for the things you listed above and enjoy having the anxiety simply melt away.

Now that you have assessed your personal heart damage, identified the causes, chosen to forgive, praised your way through various circumstances and thanked God for your blessings, you are ready to attack specific **Either/Or** thoughts with the Word of God. The chart below demonstrates how this is done.

Either/Or Thought

I can **Either** do this **Or** that but not both.

The Word's Response

I can do all things through Christ who strengthens me. (Phil. 4:13 NKJV)

Either my circumstances change **Or** I will never be happy.

Delight yourself also in the LORD, and He
Shall give you the desires of your heart. (Ps. 37:4 NKJV)

I can **Either** figure out a solution on my own **Or** this problem will never go away.

Trust in the Lord with all your heart; do not depend on your own understanding. Seek his will in all you do, and he will show you which path to take. (Prov. 3:5-6 NLT

I can **Either** hustle now and get serious about Acquiring wealth at any cost **Or** I will be poor.

Seek the Kingdom of God above all else,
And live righteously, and he will give you
Everything you need."(Matthew 6:33 NLT)

Now it is your turn. In the boxes on the left, list your **Either/Or** thoughts, and then in the box directly across from it on the right, list a Scripture to combat it.

Either/Or Thought	What the Word Says

Now you are equipped. So moving forward, anytime one of those **Either/Or** thoughts sneaks up on you, fight back and say your Scriptures aloud. Why should you say it aloud? Good question.

Well, for one thing, it's important that you hear yourself saying it (especially if you're quoting the Word) because faith comes by hearing and hearing by the Word of God (Rom. 10:17). And secondly, Satan, is not a mind reader. God is all-knowing or omniscient; the devil is not. So he can't hear you attacking his negative thoughts if you don't do so aloud.

If you say nothing, he'll get encouraged, assuming his assault is working and the thoughts will continue to come at an even faster, stronger, regular pace. Remember, if we resist the devil, he will flee, but not if we ignore and tolerate him. (James 4:7)

Let him know that you are alert and vigilant; that you recognize what he's attempting to do and pierce him through with the sword of the Spirit being released from your mouth, which is the Word of God. (Heb. 4:12)

Chapter 10: The Power Is In My Mouth

Introduction

This chapter will help you to use your mouth to slay the enemy and propel yourself forward.

"Your words can be as satisfying as fruit, as pleasing as the food that fills your stomach. The tongue can speak words that bring life or death. Those who love to talk must be ready to accept what it brings."
(Prov. 18:20-21 ERV)
"And so blessing and cursing come pouring out of the same mouth. Surely, my brothers and sisters, this is not right!" (James 3:10 NLT)

Say what you want, not what you don't want!

Overview

In order to see transformation, we need to say what we want, not what we don't want. King David made a covenant with his eyes to ensure he wouldn't sin against God and you need to make a covenant with your mouth. Vow to stop talking down to yourself, your situation, and your future. Be like God—create your world with the words of your mouth. If you read the creation story detailed in the book of Genesis, you will see repeatedly that God would say and then He would see what He said. You were created in His image and likeness so likewise, when you say something you will see it happen whether what you said was good or bad.

You Think It.

You Speak It.

You See It.

You don't fight thoughts with thoughts. You fight thoughts with words.
Sean R. Moore

Exercises

Exercise 1: In Chapter 8, Exercise 1, you listed your dreams.

   a) Now, you will take what you wrote there and create faith statements below.
   b) List Scripture references to support your faith statement.
   c) You can list as many as needed and you can write them out completely if you would like. An example has been provided to guide you.

For example:

My dream: Seeing all of my kids graduate from college

Faith Statement: All of my children will graduate from college in a reasonable amount of time with honors, knowing what their purpose is and actively walking in it. They will not have large student loans and will live debt free all of their days. The steps of a righteous man are ordered of the Lord and He will supply all of my needs according to His riches in glory by Christ Jesus (Ps. 37:23; Phil. 4:19).

Dream 1: _____
Faith Statement:_____
_____
_____

Dream 2: _____
Faith Statement:_____
_____
_____

Dream 3: _____
Faith Statement:_____
_____
_____

Dream 4: _____
Faith Statement:_____
_____
_____

Dream 5: _____
Faith Statement:_____
_____
_____

Dream 6: _____
Faith Statement:_____
_____
_____

Dream 7: _____
Faith Statement:_____
_____
_____

Dream 8: _____
Faith Statement:_____
_____
_____

Dream 9: _____
Faith Statement:_____
_____
_____

Dream 10: _____
Faith Statement:_____
_____
_____

Dream 11: _____
Faith Statement:_____
_____
_____

Dream 12: _____
Faith Statement:_____
_____
_____

Dream 13: _____
Faith Statement:_____
_____
_____

Dream 14: _____
Faith Statement:_____
_____
_____

Dream 15: _____
Faith Statement:_____
_____
_____

Dream 16: _____
Faith Statement:_____
_____
_____

Dream 17: _____
Faith Statement:_____
_____
_____

Dream 18: _____
Faith Statement:_____
_____
_____

Dream 19: _____
Faith Statement:_____
_____
_____

Dream 20: _____
Faith Statement:_____
_____
_____

And the Lord answered me, and said, write the vision, and make it plain upon tables,
that he may run that readeth it.
(Hab. 2:2 KJV)

Exercise 2: Read your faith statements every day for 30 days before going to bed. You can accompany them with the confessions you will write in the next chapter.

Challenge: Read them in the morning and or in the middle of the day as well.

Chapter 11: Confessions

Since you have been practicing saying the Word, let's continue along those lines. Below are some confessions that I have created in different categories for you to speak over your life. Following those are blank pages so that you can create your own. Create as many as you would like. You can use the faith statements you have already written. If you put them together, you should be able to create a power-packed paragraph. There are more pages available in the back of the workbook.

Confessions

Healing

With long life You will satisfy me and show me Your salvation—healing, wholeness, deliverance and preservation. My body functions the way you created it to from the foundation of the world. I prosper and I am in good health and my mind, will and emotions constantly prosper and improve. I have the mind of Christ; it is sharp, alert, remembers details, and is full of peace and trust in God. Because of what Jesus did for me on the cross, I am healed from all sicknesses and diseases. I am not afraid of what might happen to me physically. I take care of the temple He has blessed me with, and I trust Him to bless my food and water. (3 John 1:2; 1 Cor. 2:16; Isa. 53:5; Ex. 23:25)

Finances

God supplies all of my needs according to His riches in glory by Christ Jesus. He has given me richly all things to enjoy. He has given me power to get wealth. If I lack wisdom, I ask God and He gives it to me liberally without holding back. (Phil. 4:19; 1 Tim. 6:17; Deut. 8:18; James 1:5)

Protection

I live under the shadow of God almighty. I am safe in the arms of His love. I am free from fear and walk in wisdom and faith. He rescues me from every trap. I will not be afraid of disasters, terrors, or diseases. Evil cannot touch me. I am the blessed of the Lord. (Ps. 91)

Thought Life

1) I choose to think BIG thoughts. My mind works for me, not against me. I concentrate on what is true just, pure, and lovely. I don't focus on the bad. I focus on the good. Because I think good thoughts, good things always show up in my life. I am full of peace. I am full of strength. I am full of love. I am done with **Either/Or** thinking for good. (1 Cor. 2:16; Phil. 4:8; John 14:27)

2) Today, I choose to reject thoughts that fight against my understanding of God's love and goodness. I will focus on thoughts that are just and good, worthy of praise, and lovely. I will allow the thoughts and attitudes of Christ to become my own. I will cooperate with Holy Spirit in this process for the rest of my life. I thank You Lord in advance for the masterpiece that's being formed in my mind and for the masterpiece You are creating in my life. (2 Cor. 10:5; Phil. 4:8; Phil. 2:5)

3) Thank You God for Your goodness, provision, mercy and grace. I will focus on what I do like and not on what I don't like. I will focus on my blessings, and I will not take them for granted. I am in great expectation for what my future holds. I choose to let Your thoughts become my own, and I thank You in advance for the BIG LIFE I will live. I THINK BIG. I LIVE BIG. (1 Thess. 5:18; Phil 2:5; Prov. 23:7)

4) Lord I choose to empty myself of anything unlike You to make You BIG in my life. Today I choose to reject thoughts that fight against My understanding of Your Love and goodness towards me. I will focus on thoughts that are just and good, worthy of praise, and lovely. I will allow the thoughts and attitudes of Christ to become my own. I will cooperate with Holy Spirit in this process for the rest of my life. I thank You Lord in advance for the masterpiece that's being formed in my mind and for the masterpiece You are creating in my life. (Ps 51:10; 2 Cor. 10:5; Phil 2:5; 4:8, 1 Thess. 5:18-19)

Love

God is in love with me.
He is pleased with me.
He is content with me.
He is in awe of me.
(1 John 4:9-10)

Faith

1) God has forgiven me. I forgive me, too. My circumstances that are unfavorable are temporary and subject to change. This small trouble is only for a moment, and it is working for me. I will rejoice, because Christ has overcome the world. Therefore, I have already won. (2 Cor. 4:17; 5:21, John 16:33)

2) I can do all things through Christ which strengthens me. His strength is made perfect in my weakness. When I seem weak that's really when I'm strong. I am stronger than my enemy the devil. He's been defeated. I will not let him have my imagination. Instead, I yield my thoughts, my heart, my plans, and my mouth to God. I trust in Him with my whole heart, and I will not be disappointed. He died to give me an abundant & satisfying life, and I will begin living that life right now! I have the mind of Christ and I'm DONE with Either/Or thinking! (Phil. 4:13, 2 Cor. 2:16; 12:9, Prov. 3:5, John 10:10)

3) I am a person of unwavering faith created in God's image and likeness. I choose to speak words of life and not of death. I renounce every negative word spoken over me by myself and others. I choose to believe what God says. Just like Jesus I am full of the Spirit and power and will do the work of God Who has called me. I rely on your grace and the help of the Holy Spirit I declare that my life will bring you honor and glory, and because of these things I really do LOVE MY LIFE! (Gen 1:27, Deut. 30:19, Prov. 31:26, Ps. 141:3)

Christian Life

1) I choose to be activated by the Holy Ghost with power to destroy the works of the devil and to represent God's Kingdom. I choose to remain activated until Jesus comes to call me home. I choose to deactivate any distractions that would stop me from being salt and light in the earth. I am an activated champion for God, and I always will be! (1 John 3:8, Matt. 5:13-16)

2) I will be an uncompromising Christian. I will change this polluted culture to resemble a Kingdom Culture. I am called to be a world shaker and a history maker. I will not fall for the tricks of the devil. I am not deceived by the temptations of this ungodly culture. Because I am made in the image and likeness of God, I am full of His wisdom. I can't be fooled. I can't be stopped. I will represent God's kingdom and remove the shame from God's church. I will not be the laughingstock of unbelievers. I talk the talk, and I walk the walk. I represent holiness. I represent self-respect and respect for others. I carry myself in dignity I won't be stained by the sin in this world. (Ps. 92:12, 1 Pet. 5:8, Gen. 1:27, 2 Cor. 5:21)

Identity

1) I have been chosen by the King to be an ambassador of Heaven. I accept my assignment. And I accept my Helper, the Holy Spirit who has sealed me and teaches me the ways of the Kingdom. I refuse to walk in guilt or shame, because I have confessed my faults, and my King has cleansed me of all wrongdoing. Therefore, I forgive myself, and I will not live condemned but free. I will hold my head up high not in arrogance but in confidence. Because just like Jesus, I know who I am. I know where I came from, and I know where I'm going. I am the righteousness of God in Christ Jesus. I am the head and not the tail. I am above and not beneath. Everything I set my hand to is blessed. I desire to fulfill the will of my King, and He ensures that all of my needs are met. He gives me the desires of my heart. Because I delight in Him, I seek first God's Kingdom, and everything I need is freely added. My aim is to do the will of my King and to finish His work. He never leaves me alone, because I always do the things that please Him. The devil is a defeated foe. He has no claim to me, and I have nothing in common with him. I am free from sin and death, and I am empowered to represent the Kingdom. And that's exactly what I do. (1 Pet 2:9, Eph. 4:30, 1 John 1:9, 2 Cor. 5:21, Deut. 28:1-13, Ps. 37:4, Matt. 6:33, Rom. 8:2)

2) I can do all things through Christ who strengthens me. I am capable and confident, not in my own strength and abilities but in God's grace and God's promises. I am grateful and thankful to be a child of God. I will live with grace, skill, and inside information straight from the throne of God given to me by the Holy Spirit. I have an unction from the Holy One and know all things. I declare that I have all of the resources of Heaven at my disposal because I am a child of the king, and I will always be provided for. (Phil. 4:13, 1 John 2:20, Rom. 8:16-18)

Household

My household is always protected. We abide under the shadow of the almighty. We won't cower around in fear, guilt, or shame but will rise to our destinies in God's timing. We will bring glory to His name, I will lift my eyes to the Lord. I will always trust in Him. He is my constant help and hope in trouble. My steps are directed by God. He leads Me to the ways of life, prosperity, joy and fulfillment.! (Ps. 91, Ps. 37:23)

Exercise

Exercise 1: Use the lines below to create your own confession. You can make as many as you want. You may mix the categories or keep them separate as shown above. More space is provided in the end of the workbook.

Chapter 12: The Power Of Visualization

Introduction
This chapter's goal is to help you get a mental picture and maybe even a physical picture of the dream God has for you. Magic happens when your dream and His dream match. When God had big plans for Abram, He told him to visualize the dream.

Overview

Then the Lord took Abram outside and said to him, 'Look up into the sky and count the stars if you can. That's how many descendants you will have! (Gen. 15:5)

The first thing God said to Abram was "look." He gave him an image that he would see every single night to remind him of the promise He made to make him the father of many nations. What has God promised you? What picture can you look at daily to keep you focused on the promise?"

Exercises

Exercise 1: Go back to Exercise 1 in Chapter 8 and review the dreams you said you were looking forward to. On the spaces provided, list images or symbols you can look at to encourage you to stay in faith concerning your dreams.

Dream 1:_____

Image _____

Dream 2:_____

Image _____

Dream 3:_____

Image _____

Dream 4:_____

Image _____

Dream 5:_____

Image _____

Dream 6:_____

Image _____

Dream 7: _____

Image _____

Dream 8: _____

Image _____

Dream 9: _____

Image _____

Dream 10: _____

Image _____

Dream 11: _____

Image _____

Dream 12: _____

Image _____

Dream 13: _____

Image _____

Dream 14: _____

Image _____

Dream 15: _____

Image _____

Dream 16: _____

Image _____

Dream 17: _____

Image _____

Dream 18: _____

Image _____

Dream 19:_____

Image _____

Dream 20:_____

Image _____

Exercise 2:

a) Get some magazines or break out a camera and cut out pictures of what you want and tape them in the space provided that correspond with the dreams and images listed above.

b) If you want to go the extra mile, attach Scriptures next to it. You can also create a mission or proclamation statement. If the space provided isn't enough, get a poster board, binder or anything that suits you.

c) Put it somewhere you can see it daily and set a time every day to affirm and command what you see on the page to become a reality.

Now unto him that is able to do exceeding abundantly above all that we ask or think, according to the power that worketh in us. (Eph. 3:20)

The Lord answered me, "Write down what I show you. Write it clearly on a sign so that the message will be easy to read."
(Hab. 2:2 ERV)

Now to Him Who, by (in consequence of) the [action of His] power that is at work within us, is able to [carry out His purpose and] do superabundantly, far over and above all that we [dare]ask or think [infinitely beyond our highest prayers, desires, thoughts, hopes, or dreams]
(Eph. 3:20 AMPC)

Dream 1:

_____
_____
_____
_____
_____
_____
_____
_____
_____
_____
_____
_____
_____
_____
_____
_____
_____
_____
_____

Scripture reference(s):
_____

Dream 2:

_____
_____
_____
_____
_____
_____
_____
_____
_____
_____
_____
_____
_____
_____
_____
_____
_____
_____

Scripture reference(s):
_____

Dream 3:

_____

_____

_____

_____

_____

_____

_____

_____

_____

_____

_____

_____

_____

_____

_____

_____

_____

Scripture reference(s):

_____

Dream 4:

_____

_____

_____

_____

_____

_____

_____

_____

_____

_____

_____

_____

_____

_____

_____

_____

Scripture reference(s):

_____

Dream 5:

_____
_____
_____
_____
_____
_____
_____
_____
_____
_____
_____
_____
_____
_____
_____
_____
_____
_____
_____
_____
_____
_____
_____

Scripture reference(s):
_____

Dream 6:

_____
_____
_____
_____
_____
_____
_____
_____
_____
_____
_____
_____
_____
_____
_____
_____
_____
_____
_____

Scripture reference(s):
_____

Dream 7:

_____
_____
_____
_____
_____
_____
_____
_____
_____
_____
_____
_____
_____
_____
_____
_____
_____
_____
_____
_____
_____

Scripture reference(s):
_____

Dream 8:

_____
_____
_____
_____
_____
_____
_____
_____
_____
_____
_____
_____
_____
_____
_____
_____
_____

Scripture reference(s):
_____

Dream 9:

_____
_____
_____
_____
_____
_____
_____
_____
_____
_____
_____
_____
_____
_____
_____
_____
_____
_____
_____
_____
_____
_____

Scripture reference(s):
_____

Dream 10:

_____
_____
_____
_____
_____
_____
_____
_____
_____
_____
_____
_____
_____
_____
_____
_____
_____
_____
_____
_____
_____

Scripture reference(s):
_____

Dream 11:

_____
_____
_____
_____
_____
_____
_____
_____
_____
_____
_____
_____
_____
_____
_____
_____
_____
_____
_____

Scripture reference(s):
_____

Dream 12:

_____
_____
_____
_____
_____
_____
_____
_____
_____
_____
_____
_____
_____
_____
_____
_____
_____
_____
_____

Scripture reference(s):
_____

Dream 13:

_____

_____

_____

_____

_____

_____

_____

_____

_____

_____

_____

_____

_____

_____

_____

_____

_____

_____

_____

_____

_____

Scripture reference(s):

_____

Dream 14:

_____

_____

_____

_____

_____

_____

_____

_____

_____

_____

_____

_____

_____

_____

_____

_____

_____

_____

Scripture reference(s):

_____

Dream 15:

_____
_____
_____
_____
_____
_____
_____
_____
_____
_____
_____
_____
_____
_____
_____
_____
_____
_____
_____
_____
_____

Scripture reference(s):
_____

Dream 16:

_____
_____
_____
_____
_____
_____
_____
_____
_____
_____
_____
_____
_____
_____
_____
_____
_____
_____

Scripture reference(s):
_____

Dream 17:

_____
_____
_____
_____
_____
_____
_____
_____
_____
_____
_____
_____
_____
_____
_____
_____
_____
_____
_____

Scripture reference(s):
_____

Dream 18:

_____
_____
_____
_____
_____
_____
_____
_____
_____
_____
_____
_____
_____
_____
_____
_____
_____
_____
_____

Scripture reference(s):
_____

Dream 19:

_____

_____

_____

_____

_____

_____

_____

_____

_____

_____

_____

_____

_____

_____

_____

_____

_____

_____

_____

Scripture reference(s):

_____

Dream 20:

_____

_____

_____

_____

_____

_____

_____

_____

_____

_____

_____

_____

_____

_____

_____

Scripture reference(s):

_____

Chapter 13: Final Thoughts

Congratulations! You have made it through the entire workbook. Only you know if you skipped through some exercises to get to some others. I will not judge your process, but I do recommend that you go back and fill out the ones you haven't completed yet. Also, the chapters that proved to be the most painful or difficult for you to complete, take that information to God in prayer. You might want to share with a friend, loved one, or a counselor. You are well on your way to obtaining and maintaining a healthy mind for the long haul. This is great news because you are what you think!

For as he thinks in his heart, so is he. (Prov. 23:7a AMPC)

The Most Important Thing You'll Ever Do

God loves you. Yes, you! In spite of your flaws and circumstances and past, He loves you. He loves you so much that He sent His Son Jesus to die on a cross for you thousands of years before you were even born knowing that you might reject Him. He still thought you were worth the sacrifice and so do I. Please do me the honor of allowing me to walk you through what many call the sinner's prayer. I like to call it the salvation prayer.

But what does it say? "The word is near you, in your mouth and in your heart" (that is, the word of faith which we preach): that if you confess with your mouth the Lord Jesus and believe in your heart that God has raised Him from the dead, you will be saved. For with the heart one believes unto righteousness, and with the mouth confession is made unto salvation.
(Rom. 10:8–10 NKJV)

Based on this Scripture, if you believe in your heart that Jesus died for your sin and you say that with your mouth, you are saved! Saved from what? From sin and its penalty. The wages of sin is death. Not just death physical, but emotional, spiritual, and any other way. Ultimately, sin separates us from God. Our source of life. And if you'd like to be reconnected to your life source, say this aloud:

Heavenly Father, I believe that Jesus was sent by God to earth to die for my sins and that He rose from the dead. Thank you God for providing a savior for me so long ago. I receive Jesus today as my savior. Thank you for saving me from sin and its penalty. Thank you for wiping my slate clean and adopting me into your family. I am now a child of God. I am so grateful, and I trust you Holy Spirit to lead me as I develop into a mature believer. Amen.

Congratulations! If you prayed that prayer, you are now a born-again child who is adopted into God's family. Here are some Scripture references to help you understand what has taken place.

Therefore, if anyone is in Christ, he is a new creation; old things have passed away; behold, all things have become new. Now all things are of God, who has reconciled us to Himself through Jesus Christ, and has given us the ministry of reconciliation, that is, that God was in Christ reconciling the world to Himself, not imputing their trespasses to them, and has committed to us the word of reconciliation. Now then, we are ambassadors for Christ, as though God were pleading through us: we implore you on Christ's behalf, be reconciled to God. For He made Him who knew no sin to be sin for us, that we might become the righteousness of God in Him.
(2 Cor. 5:17–21 NKJV)

For you did not receive the spirit of bondage again to fear, but you received the Spirit of adoption by whom we cry out, "Abba, Father." The Spirit Himself bears witness with our spirit that we are children of God, and if children, then heirs—heirs of God and joint heirs with Christ, if indeed we suffer with Him, that we may also be glorified together.
(Rom. 8:15–17)

If you prayed this prayer for the first time or you prayed it again because you've strayed away from God but have returned, please let me know by visiting my website at www.EricaRenee.co. I would love to celebrate with you. I also recommend that you get a Bible or Bible App that you will read or listen to and join a local church that will teach you the Bible and help you to grow in your Christian walk. God bless you!

About the Author

Erica Renée is a proud wife and mother of four beautiful children. She and her husband, Sean R. Moore, pastor a thriving church in Phoenix, AZ, Faith Christian Center. They met at Michigan State University, where she graduated with a BA in Communication. Erica is a licensed and ordained minister and has been a Christ follower since she was a young child.

Erica's teaching is packed with life-enhancing truths and delivered with humor and simplicity at church services, events, various media outlets and conferences. She is the founder of the women's ministry, Woman2Woman and the W2W book club. Her goal is to empower men and women to be their best as she writes and speaks the truth in love.

To find out more about her products and for booking and or speaking dates, you can visit her website at www.EricaRenee.co. If you would like information regarding Woman2Woman, the book club, or Faith Christian Center, please visit www.fcc-phx.com

Notes:

Made in the USA
Monee, IL
08 April 2024